YOUR FLAME PERFORMS

A collection of poetry by William Colucci

Your Flame Performs ©

**Copyright,
William Colucci,
2010**

**I.S.B.N.
978-0-9866436-0-6**

NOTICE: The hyperlinks provided do not work with all readers of Lulu.com e-books

1 "PROEM"; THE AUTHOR'S FORWARD

2 MY TIMES

3 MISTRESS OF SPACE

4 SHADOW

5 HERE WE ARE

6 NATURAL AFFECTION

7 LYING IN THE DARK

8 SHE YAWNS

9 INTIMIDATED

10 BESIDE HER BODY

11 MOTION

12 SHE TURNS BETWEEN MAY ARMS

13 I QUESTION EVERYTHING

14 STOP HER SHE IS TOO BEAUTIFUL

15 I REFUSE

16 LONESOME STORIES

17 IF I READ TO YOU

18 NIGHT LASH

19 BACK DAWN

20 THROUGH STREETS

21 THE RAGING BROW OF DAWN

22 SOFT LIVERY

23 PASSION

24 TRUST ME

25 THE STARS IN HER EYES

26 I HAVE THE LAST FLOWER

27 I DREAM

28 WE HAVE OUR DRESDENS

29 ROXANA

30 I KNOW YOU ARE BEAUTIFUL

31 I COULD SEDUCE THE WORLD

32 HER EYES

33 THE LADY IN THE MIRROR

34 ANOTHER POEM

35 IF YOU PASS

36 I WAIT

37 TO YOU

38 YOU BEAUTIFUL WOMEN

39 THE BONDS OF BEAUTY

40 FUNNY

1 "PROEM" THE AUTHOR'S FORWARD

Beyond the dream
lies the consequence of fact,
the bite of truth, which digs without twist,
impales without flinch;
it is the inescapable reality,
palpable and stoic,
resonant as pain.

The ever presence of truth
cannot be shed as the dream,
feathered and deformed,
continually optimistic;
born with fairy wings
and satyr's hooves it flies beyond hope,
passing reason and logic
in bounds.

The mind of dreams alone leaves a cold
catatonic corpse,
while the heart without,
being of fact enthralled
and beyond enlightenment
is more cold than death.

2 MY TIMES

I have my times
as Hitler and Mussolini had theirs,
but my times are times of solitude
when the crowd hides away.

I am the Crusoe of my apartment block,
and for a vocal parrot I have my radio reality,
ever echoing bare walls in endless circles,
back forth, back forth;
not unlike the barber's mirrored walls,
seeing past my thousand shoulders
an ever shrinking countenance.

I have my times, the last slow ripples
when the stone has sunk, riding in silence,
waiting for eternity to smooth over
and forget I passed.

Some have moments like the last dying star flare,
beacons crying from Texas towers,
or smoldering on street corners.

But my times are quiet,
like birds sleeping on still air
my separate reality turns slowly
to the tune of circling stars.

3 MISTRESS OF SPACE

Night is her gown
breath close,
moonlight train
crossing space.
She rides,
pale in darkness
eye of a thousand lovers;
she saw the pride and humiliation of Helen,
Romeo's birth and pain.
Love letters by thousands
poetry in flames
praise her grace,
mother of beauty
mistress of space.

4 SHADOW

I would I could
show my shadow
in the stead
of my flatterless features
where friends
amidst the throng
could read
where light breaks through
and the tartan patchwork
where others made light
of my translucence.

5 <u>HERE WE ARE</u>

Here we are
your blue silence
my long neck
and wind

What if rain
you gray in youth
I hang below
melting eyes

What if night
black modesty
ink on ink in dark

Here we are
your bright eyes
my long silence
and wind.

6 NATURAL AFFECTION

Come stand beside an autumn tree,
October breath coloring your words,
late sun – hiding;
burdened limbs drop mottled tears
about your feet,
fleeing the wind's vile temperament – they pause
to kiss your ankles tenderly
and are gone in frenzied madness;
while adulating limbs, I bow,
shed chipped amber tears
and turn my head to dreams
of white solitude.

7 LYING IN THE DARK

Lying in the dark
she is a small desert,
and I, her suffering explorer,
my hands, caravans,
weave through scenery;
her hills stand white
untouched mountains,
her valleys secret.

How many have died
crossing this woman?
I have died crossing her.
I have given my breath
to every inch of her body,
and retrieving it slowly,
have learned her lands
as Alexander learned Persia.

8 SHE YAWNS

How she yawns
like the sea.
Stretching smooth limbs
to the edge of vision;
catching her white form
against the night,
no mean trick
in darkness,
she flows
beneath the sheets.

9 INTIMIDATED

I am intimidated
by her innocence,
beauty, splendor
and all the contrasts
of womanhood.

I fear her touch
that I may compromise
the purity I revere

And though know
her mortal
know also
we have conquered
the carnal instinct.

10 BESIDE HER BODY

Beside her body
I am dumb to mouth
the pleasantries
such lovers perform;
the ritual over, all words fail
the justice of her beauty
and her beauty fails
the justice of her body;

and I can only
sacrifice my mouth to hers,
bless her lips and ears
and crawl close beside
this solitary soul,
a penitent without
the mission of her body.

11 **MOTION**

Earth in motion
she moves beneath me
her dew
settling our sheets

Her smooth thighs
ritualize love
with enchanting motions
of pagans
or virgins
touched in sleep

Her small breasts
beneath my chest
shame past lovers
of centerfold proportions
with gentle heaves
of sparrow's breath
they move with all
the innocence of love.

12 SHE TURNS BETWEEN MY ARMS

The pale eye of time sleeps
suspended
beards gray between cricket chirps
dust grows into mountains
she turns between my arms.

Dynasties are slaughtered
continents subdued by seas
mountains turn to dust
and she turns between my arms.

13   I QUESTION EVERYTHING

I question everything
except this woman.
There are no starving children,
no hunger,
no pestilence.
There is only her dark eyes
which I love with all
the ignorance of flesh.

There are no wars,
no fanatics
plotting our destruction,
no time
plotting our entombment.
There is only the black river
of her hair
and my sailor's hand
on her soft nape.

There is no day to come,
no dawn,
not light,
only this long night
to wrap around us
with all the consequence
of mortality.

14 STOP HER; SHE IS TOO BEAUTIFUL

Stop her:
she is too beautiful.
The romance of her eyes
denies my sight
the failures of mortal visage.

She is too radiant:
she blinds my heart
with unequalled splendor
of lips and flesh
and all the arts
which mesh in womanhood.

15 I REFUSE

I refuse to believe
there is more beauty
beyond the dark
that light can flaunt
what night denies
that touch reveals
less beauty than the eyes.

I doubt the glamour
of her at night
can be enhanced
by mere daylight
that there is a greater
work of art
than this deft
and loving heart.

16 LONESOME STORIES

Lonesome stories hang,
half frozen tears
from a widowed eye;
lover's bent flesh
feeds roses
in the dark.
The unseen worm
curling within
a blossom,
cries crimson
with dawn's
first strike,
and with the rising
lid of night
spawns wings and flight.

17 IF I READ TO YOU

If I read to you
from my long book
will you close the night
for a while;
pull it down
around our horizons,
down
to where the river
cuts the beach,
and tuck it in
gently
where flesh is tender
and dew thick?

If I give you one more story
you must promise
to accept the dark,
fluff it, if you will
beneath your dreams
and curl
within its folds;
you are safe,
dawn is hours
away.

18 NIGHT LASH

Her night lash
tickles close,
teases my cheek awake.
Where eye light waivers
across horizon lid,
bloom's deep light
through petal curtain peeps;
with sun shy wings
it fades and doe-like sleeps.

19 BACK DAWN

Back dawn back,
he sleeps yet
and in sleep perchance
finds peace from this
relentless lover
who like the raging sea
beats down
upon this frail form,
this ivory bust,
which shook like a leaf
beneath the storm.

Light fail to break upon this curtain,
upon this sheet,
which like a shroud
envelopes all of grace
within my world,
within this place
and fail to shine
within this room
where this woman child
gently lies.

Return oh night
you are our ken,
shall be our final
resting place,
where a sleeping
and a doting soul
will lay forever

in your dark heart,
where sleeping is
the better part
of love and of
love's art.

20 THROUGH STREETS

Through streets
my eyes have followed women
whom Michael Angelo
would have loved
without his chisel,
who walked lightly
in the dark
and had balanced
paperbacks
on their heads,
but when they spoke
butterflies behind their teeth
growled.

21 THE RAGING BROW OF DAWN

The bird who beats the raging brow of dawn
beats my green years
to the yellow gorge,
red lips crying for distant nights;
bemoaning dying of the light,
when the voice that calls
the golden grain
calls for answers with my name
and when my eyes will fail to see,
I'll spend the dark in dreams of thee.

22 SOFT LIVERY

Drawn long from ivory
in the soft livery of her own smooth flesh
she shames the night;
moon pale and bright
the orbs of her breasts
suspend my light breath
and calm the air about her.

Long etched limbs
lie still and stretched
by her fair sides
which coolly hide her flame
which we tamed so soon ago.

23 PASSION

Love me
with all the passion
at your command
or not at all.
There are times
when flesh alone
is not enough
and abstinence
will not suffice.

There are nights
which close like
a continent subdued
by a world of ice
and eyes
which melt the night,
shade the day
and steal this
aching heart away.

24 TRUST ME

Don't trust the night,
it ends before delight.

Don't trust the day,
it soon will go away.

Trust me,
I'm here and will always be.

25 THE STARS IN HER EYES

The last time I counted
the stars in her eyes,
I held fast my chair
for fear of falling
into their dark pools,
where fish
with golden lanterns swim
and sirens sing enchantments
through the dark.

Like Alice,
I would have crossed beyond
those mirrored planes,
but to where lotus eaters sleep
and play inward games
upon hearts
of heathen sailors;
though the innocence she bore
of my affection
bade me bear my heart
in silence.

Now when in darkness
I repair,
I dream that again
I am there,
in her eye of night.

26 I HAVE THE LAST FLOWER

I have the last flower
which slipped gently
from her smile's seam,
her cheek pressed against
the door frame,
she watched the hallway,
cruel cavern,
consume my departure.

Trailing her vision,
silver streamers
growing upon the air,
I suffered a chaste farewell,
yet, seed or amber,
the scene remains
etched beyond my mind's tablet,
tabloid of a thousand
painful revisions.

27 I DREAM

I dream
with every movement
of your mouth
that we are lovers

that this fair day
is carved from eternity
for us alone

that I am lost
in the task of learning
the infinity of your body.

28 WE HAVE OUR DRESDENS

We have our Dresdens,
china figures among the cinders,
in the name of harsh gray gods
we mete out hell,
bless the saints,
cure the atrocities of our enemies
and ignore the Nagasaki children.

Our flowers are withered,
their scorched petals writhe
on alters dry with blood
and dust in the dusk
of our innocence.

There is no flood
behind our fires,
no pillars of salt
save dust.

We have our Dresdens.

29 ROXANA

Be to me an effigy
while I portray in art
the smiles and shams which betray a man's
relinquishing his heart.

Your shy eyes don't realize
the potency of their charm,
the way they fire
a man's desire
and raise his heart's alarm;

For 'tis I who stand at your command
loving every grace
about your warm and gentle form
and flowing o'er your face,

But if perchance you catch my glance
and deem it more than mild,
please never fear
upon drawing near
my ambitions are too wild.

For no soul knows what heart throes
another suffers through,
blood's hot course,
the mind's divorce,
a vanity cast for two.

30 I KNOW YOU ARE BEAUTIFUL

I know you are beautiful;
your eyes shout it at me,
perhaps it is my desire
that makes them so blue
and your lips so red,
or was it some sardonic god
who hates all men
and has chosen you
to punish their loins
and lips with abstinence.

If I touch you in the dark
don't fear my flesh
it is all a sacrifice
of the lion to the lamb,
though when it is over
you will realize
my love is a libation
at the altar of your beauty.

31 I COULD SEDUCE THE WORLD

I could seduce the world,
but I will start
with this woman.

With her lips which purse
like fine red portals
and call me master
of the night.

With her eyes which shine
like golden beacons
guiding my sailor's soul
to their black depths,

and the pillars of her thighs
which so slightly tremble
as I touch the port of Venus.

32 HER EYES

I desire your eyes,
your lips, breasts
and body,
but most of all
your eyes.

With less compassion
than a sailor in heat
I plan their conquest,
not for good or evil
but for tonight;
for the ardor of love
not bound by flesh
and flesh not bound
by shame

And when the longing
sleeps within our loins
I will still have
your eyes to love.

33 THE LADY IN THE MIRROR

The lady in the mirror
is the mirror,
she lives beyond the crystal plane
in the religion of her flesh,
the holy ivory she caresses
with oils and powders
and perfumes the air
with the decorum of a priest.

In the shrine of her eyes
lies her fidelity,
a nymph of Venus
at her altar,
prepared to sacrifice
a thousand lives
to her enticements.

34 **<u>ANOTHER POEM</u>**

For you who don't want
another poem,
I am dedicating:

2 X-rays of Goebbles chest
3 Stains from a reputed crucifixion
1 Map of Hiroshima (before)
2 Cinders from Hiroshima (after)

And every curse spoken
since I wrote this.

35 IF YOU PASS

If you pass by the thighs
where my lady gives,
check in her eyes
see if she lives.

Are the whites still as bright
as headlamps at night?
Is the green as enchanting
as leprechauns dancing?

Is there flesh on her bone?
Are her lips still as red,
or does she moan with the tone
of the dying and dead?

36 I WAIT

I wait for you lady comfort
come to me for a while
with your heartaches and your darkness
and the cancer in your smile.

I wait for my lady shadow
where the river meets the road
and the pedestrians all gather
to lighten up their load.

I await my lady darkness
where the sun cannot see
where little feet scurry
on the passage to the sea.

I await my lady evermore
in my hole beneath the sod
I await her for eternities
for a demon or a god.

37 TO YOU

To you who believe
Auschwitz and Hiroshima
were sores
we will grow over,
that Nero was mad,
(only because he burned Rome)
that cannibals are savages
who eat in ignorance.

To you,
I can talk about
rainbows
and razor blades,
Easter eggs
and the dark diseases
of lovers and whores;

but you won't hear,
you have mastered the eternal echo.

38 YOU BEAUTIFUL WOMEN

This is for
you beautiful women
who want a poet
by your bedstead,
to whisper into your ear,
that is like a rose,
you love is breath
and your body
a pool
by which
he may consult
or bathe.

This is for
your fantasy
that I can make you happier
than a doctor
or butcher.

39 THE BONDS OF BEAUTY

I damn the bonds of beauty
which wrap about my sight,
with serpentine coils,
elusive foils
and treachery of the light.

A man survives by duty,
a woman by her wiles
great power lies
in those eyes
and in those artful smiles.

What ladies do ensure
is their best defense
has been used
and been abused
with every false pretense;

but when a soul is pure
and innocence survives,
there is no doubt,
from within or out,
we love them all our lives,

for a love both deep and sound
will lead a man toward
the woman's heart,
which is the part,
which bears it own reward,

and when that love is bound
within a holy place
you can be sure
that love is pure,
and blessed with God's good grace.

40 FUNNY

Funny you should ask
what lights my heart
while your flame performs
gentle pirouettes in dark.

www.ingramcontent.com/pod-product-compliance
Lightning Source LLC
LaVergne TN
LVHW011431080426
835512LV00005B/379